This book belongs to

_____

For my parents, John and Melanie Tappen

© 2019 Alexis Merrill

All rights reserved. No part of this book may be reproduced in any form or by any means without permission in writing from the publisher, Deseret Book Company, at permissions@deseretbook.com or PO Box 30178, Salt Lake City, Utah 84130. This work is not an official publication of The Church of Jesus Christ of Latter-day Saints. The views expressed herein are the responsibility of the author and do not necessarily represent the position of the Church or of Deseret Book Company.

DESERET BOOK is a registered trademark of Deseret Book Company.

Visit us at deseretbook.com

Library of Congress Cataloging-in-Publication Data
Names: Merrill, Alexis, author.
Title: My Bible friends / Alexis Merrill.
Description: Salt Lake City, Utah : Deseret Book, [2019] | Includes bibliographical references.
Identifiers: LCCN 2019016873 | ISBN 9781629726281 (board book : alk. paper)
Subjects: LCSH: Bible—Biography—Juvenile literature. | Children—Spiritual life—Juvenile literature. | Children—Conduct of life—
    Juvenile literature. | The Church of Jesus Christ of Latter-day Saints—Conduct of life. | LCGFT: Bible stories.
Classification: LCC BS551.3 .M47 2019 | DDC 220.9/2—dc23
LC record available at https://lccn.loc.gov/2019016873

Printed in China
Four Colour Print Group, Nansha, China   6/2019

10 9 8 7 6 5 4 3 2 1

MY BIBLE FRIENDS

Written and Illustrated by Alexis Merrill

DESERET BOOK

Salt Lake City, Utah

Our Bible friends lived a long time ago. Just like you, they learned about Jesus Christ from prophets, their families, and the Holy Ghost. They had special

ATTRIBUTES that helped them be more like the Savior. Let's meet some of our Bible friends!

An ATTRIBUTE is a quality or characteristic that you have. Every one of Heavenly Father's children, including you, has positive attributes that can be like special powers.

The Savior is called the "Good Shepherd" in the Bible. Like a shepherd's flock of sheep, we follow Him. Search for a hidden sheep in each scene!

Wise like
EVE

Eve's first home was in the beautiful Garden of Eden filled with flowers, fruits, and trees. Heavenly Father and Jesus Christ visited Eve and her husband, Adam, to teach them. As they tended to the plants and animals in the garden, Eve carefully pondered Heavenly Father's commandment to have children. She and Adam chose to leave the Garden of Eden so that we could come to earth, too.

A WISE friend remembers that Heavenly Father's commandments will help us.

I am WISE like Eve when I make good choices.

Genesis 2:15-17; Moses 2:28-31; 4:6-12; 5:10-11

Diligent like
NOAH

The prophet Noah built a big boat called an ark. It was up to Noah to save Heavenly Father's creations from pouring rain that would cover the earth. Noah stocked the sturdy ark with seeds from fruits, vegetables, trees, and flowers to grow again after the flood. Animals, birds, and insects followed Noah and his family inside the ark, staying safe and dry. After many months, the water dried up and Noah's ark rested on the land.

A DILIGENT friend keeps working until a job is completed.

I am DILIGENT like Noah when I help until all the chores are done.

Genesis 6:14–22; 7:5

Forgiving like
JOSEPH

Long before Joseph became a great leader in Egypt, he lived in Canaan with his parents and eleven brothers. His jealous older brothers hated Joseph so much that they sold him to strangers traveling to Egypt. Many years later, food stopped growing, and people were starving. The hungry brothers headed to Egypt, where Joseph was helping to store food for everyone. They were surprised to see Joseph again! Joseph forgave his brothers and shared food with them.

A FORGIVING friend shows love to those who are unkind.

I am FORGIVING like Joseph when I am kind to people who have hurt my feelings.

Genesis 37:3-4, 23-28; 41:53-54; 42:2, 6-7; 45:4-5, 15

Bold like
MOSES

After escaping from Pharaoh and the Egyptians, Moses and the Israelites reached a dead end at the edge of the Red Sea. Soon, the Egyptians would catch up to them, and bring them back to Egypt as slaves. "Fear ye not . . . the Lord shall fight for you," Moses told the Israelites, as he boldly lifted his staff over the water. The deep water of the Red Sea moved apart, creating a dry path. Because of Moses's great faith, God held the water back while the Israelites safely crossed to freedom.

A BOLD friend remembers to ask Heavenly Father for help.

I am BOLD like Moses when I pray for special blessings.

Exodus 14:9–10, 13, 16, 21–22, 26

Honest like HANNAH

Hannah prayed for many years to have a baby of her own. Her prayer included a promise to Heavenly Father that her son would grow up serving Him in the temple. Hannah's prayers were answered with a baby boy she named Samuel. Though she loved her son very much, Hannah kept her promise to God. When Samuel was still a young boy, Hannah took him to live with Eli, the high priest of the temple.

An HONEST friend remembers and keeps promises, even if it is hard.

I am HONEST like Hannah when I remember the promises I have made, wherever I am.

1 Samuel 1:5-11, 20-28

Confident like
DAVID

David, a young Jewish shepherd, bravely stepped forward to fight Goliath, a Philistine warrior who stood nine feet tall! Goliath boasted that if the Jews could defeat him, then the Philistines would stop fighting and serve them. So, confident that God would help him, David faced Goliath without wearing armor or swinging a sword. With only a sling and a single, smooth stone, David killed Goliath.

A CONFIDENT friend knows that even small children can be powerful, when they depend on God.

I am CONFIDENT like David when I help others, even though I am small.

1 Samuel 17:33, 37-40, 45-46, 49

Dedicated like DEBORAH

When the Israelites needed help making decisions or getting along with each other, they visited Deborah, their wise judge and prophetess. She was dedicated to serving her people and Heavenly Father. When Deborah learned that God had given instructions for a great battle that were not followed, she took action! Deborah made a bold plan for the Israelite army to defeat their enemies and even went with them to battle. The army felt strong with Deborah guiding them.

A DEDICATED friend shows love for Heavenly Father through good choices.

I am DEDICATED like Deborah when I choose the right, even if others don't.

Judges 4:4-16

Courageous like
ESTHER

Queen Esther was married to a powerful Persian king who wanted to put all Jews to death just because they believed in God. The Jews hoped that Queen Esther, also a Jew, would stop her husband! But visiting the king's court without his permission would get Esther into trouble, or even killed. Esther risked her own safety and asked her husband to save her people. The king loved Esther, so he changed the law.

A COURAGEOUS friend speaks up to help others be happy or safe.

I am COURAGEOUS like Esther when I ask my friends to treat others nicely.

Esther 2:17; 3:13; 4:11, 16; 5:1-3; 7:3-4; 8:4-8

Steadfast like
DANIEL

Just as he had been taught as a young boy, Daniel knelt down to pray to Heavenly Father every day. But a law in Daniel's city punished people who prayed to God, so Daniel was locked in a den with hungry lions. Daniel knew that Heavenly Father would protect him because he was steadfast in saying his prayers. During the long night, the lions did not hurt Daniel.

A STEADFAST friend always obeys Heavenly Father, even if others say not to.

I am STEADFAST like Daniel when I say my prayers every day.

Daniel 6:3, 7–23

Thoughtful like
MARY AND MARTHA

Two sisters, Mary and Martha, thoughtfully ministered to their friend Jesus Christ as He taught His gospel to people everywhere. The sisters eagerly welcomed the Savior into their home. Martha hurried around, serving Jesus, while Mary sat at Jesus's feet, listening to Him teach. Even though they served Him differently, both sisters showed their love for Jesus Christ.

A THOUGHTFUL friend chooses special ways to help others.

I am THOUGHTFUL like Mary and Martha when I sit with new friends at church to make them feel welcome.

Luke 10:38–42

Generous like
THE JEWISH WIDOW

As Jesus glanced around the temple in Jerusalem, he noticed a poor Jewish widow paying her offering. Though she had only two small coins left in her pouch, the widow gave both of them away. Her offering was smaller than others, but Jesus taught His Apostles that the widow had generously shared all she had.

A GENEROUS friend shares with others to help them.

I am GENEROUS like the Jewish widow when I share what I have with my friends.

Mark 12:41-44

Humble like
PETER

Peter, a fisherman, fished all night on his boat without a single catch! As Peter was heading home, Jesus told him to put his net into the water one more time. Peter knew all about fishing, but he humbly listened to his friend. When Peter pulled the net out of the water, it was filled with so many fish that the net broke! Peter gave up being a fisherman to teach with Jesus, learning how to lead the Church after Jesus's death and resurrection.

A HUMBLE friend listens to others who are trying to help.

I am HUMBLE like Peter when I let my siblings or others teach me something new.

Matthew 4:18-20; Luke 5:1-11

Learning like ME!

Just like my Bible friends, I have special attributes that help me be more like Jesus Christ. When I am wise like Eve, forgiving like Joseph, or courageous like Esther, I feel closer to my Savior and I keep His commandments.

"My sheep hear my voice, and I know them, and they follow me." —John 10:27

About the Author

In addition to being the author and illustrator of two children's books, Alexis Tappen Merrill considers herself to be a chauffeur, nurse, teacher, editor, mediator, chef, personal shopper, and event planner! She earned degrees in chemistry and statistics from Brigham Young University, while the rest of her training came from raising four kids with her husband, Mark. Alexis and her family live in Maui, Hawaii.